3

TO PLAN, START AND COMPLETE YOUR CHILDREN'S BOOK

FLYING START STORIES

HELEN HARALDSEN

Flying Start Stories

Cover and interior design by Let's Get Booked

www.letsgetbooked.com

Paperback ISBN: 978-1-913953-14-0

eBook ISBN: 978-1-913953-15-7

There is a Workbook to Accompany this Book.

To help you put many of the ideas in this book into practice quickly, I've created a workbook to use alongside it. It's available from Amazon or free to download as a PDF by joining my mailing list from the homepage of

www.helenharaldsen.co.uk

Contents

"There is something delicious about writing the first

words of a story. You never quite know where they'll

take you."

Beatrix Potter

Introduction

Lots of people *start* to write a book, but only 3% of those people finish it. Starting a book is hard enough, but finishing it is even harder. Why is that? That's the part that interests me and the part I want to help you with.

Hello, and welcome to *Flying Start Stories*.

At the point of writing this, I'm the author of ten published children's books. I started out with a small publisher in 2019, but by 2020 I was an independent author thanks to COVID-19 causing my publisher to close. This book is a result of all the things I've read and experienced for myself over the last three years.

This book is not about 'how to write a children's book.' There are lots of books that will break down the 'how to' element, and I'll share some of my recommendations with you in the 'recommended reads' section later. It's one thing to understand the formula for writing a book and to be aware of the essential elements of a successful story. There's a world of information out there to teach the theory of it, but learning the theory is the easy part. It's the sitting down and writing the story that's the hard part. I want to help you approach the manual 'getting it done' so you can be part of the 3%.

If you're reading this book, I assume you have an interest in writing a children's book of your own. You may even have read some of the books about how to do so. If not, see my 'recommended reads'. You might have an idea for your book, and you might have started writing it. If you have, you've probably met one of the five antagonists that pit themselves against writers and try to stop them from completing that book. Those villains are:

1. Overthinking / procrastinating.
2. Perfectionism.
3. Self-doubt / imposter syndrome.
4. Commitment / time.
5. Indecision.

In my time as a developing writer, I've met and battled with all of these and I understand how each of them can have a powerful (negative) effect on writers' confidence.

It's my mission to make sure you are fully acquainted with the ways in which they present themselves so that you can recognise and brush them out of the way on your journey to writing your children's book.

So, here are some more detailed introductions:

Overthinking/Procrastination

It's easy to put off writing a book because you're still deciding what to write about. While it's a good idea to plan a story before you write it (more on this later) and to think about who it will appeal to, how you'll market it etc, sometimes the desire to write the 'perfect' book can put you off writing anything. If you have lots of different ideas, settling on one and committing to it can also be difficult. You can worry, 'is this the best story to be investing my time and effort into? Maybe one of my other ideas would be better.' This can lead to endless procrastination and indecision and stop you from ever actually getting started with writing anything at all. The more you think about it, the more you put it off because of paralysis by analysis.

"You have to write the book that wants to be written.
And if the book will be too difficult for grown-ups,
then you write it for children."

Madeleine L'Engle

Perfectionism

Similar to 'overthinking' is the worry that your book isn't perfect. It's a fact that a first draft of a story won't be perfect. It's rough, it's messy; even if you've planned it first, you're still finding your way as you go.

I know from experience how hard it is to keep sitting down to write a story that is feeling like hard work. I've learned that it's perfectly normal and lots of writers hate writing first drafts and think their story is awful to begin with. Wanting to write a perfect story in one go is pretty much impossible, but first drafts are not to be feared. During that imperfect first draft, you get to know your characters and their world. The story might start to take on a life of its own and make suggestions that weren't part of the original plan. This is part of the joy of writing.

Even when your book is finished, edited and published, it is unlikely to be perfect. Look at reviews online for some of the most loved and successful books ever published. They all have haters as well as their legions of fans. Nothing can ever appeal to everyone, so don't worry about it. Think about your ideal reader and what they'll appreciate and that'll help you get as close to 'perfect' as you can.

> "The first draft is just telling yourself the story. Write down everything that happens in the story, and then in your second draft make it look like you knew what you were doing all along."
>
>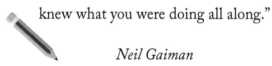
>
> *Neil Gaiman*

Self-doubt / imposter syndrome

'Who am I to be writing a book?', 'Who wants to read something I've written?', 'I can't write as well as X, Y or Z so why am I even bothering?', 'What will people think of my book? What if they don't think it's any good? What if

I get nothing but negative reviews?', 'Can I actually write?' 'It won't be good enough,' 'I'm not good enough.'

These are the questions and statements writers, including me, ask and tell themselves. It's completely normal and so long as it doesn't lead to procrastination, it's not a bad thing as it makes you do the things you need to, to silence the negative, doubting voices in your head. Remember too, the things your mind tells you aren't always true and aren't always correct. It's not deliberately trying to sabotage your dreams, it's just your brain attempting to be helpful by keeping you safe within your comfort zone.

To silence the saboteur mindset, you can thank the Doubting Thomas in your head for looking out for you, but reassure it that there's no need to worry because there are plenty of actions you can take to help you prepare to be good enough:

- research your genre to find out what's popular and why
- read the kind of books you want to write

- speak to children about what they enjoy reading

- read non-fiction books about writing

- join a writers' group

- hire an editor

- notice that all books have some negative reviews, no matter how successful they are...

Very few writers become an overnight success with their first book. Many more develop success over time as their writing improves. Many well-known authors have had their books rejected by publishers, only to go on and become worldwide best-sellers. JK Rowling had the first *Harry Potter* book turned down by 12 publishers before Bloomsbury signed her up and Stephen Kings' *Carrie* was rejected 30 times on the basis 'it wouldn't sell'. Within 12 months of publication, it sold over a million copies. Other famous examples include:

- *Dune* by Frank Herbert is the best-selling science fiction novel of all time. It's been made into a movie and won a Hugo and Nebula award, yet it faced over 20 rejections before finding a publisher.

- The Wonderful Wizard of Oz by Frank L. Baum is one of the best-known children's books of all time, yet it was rejected so many times, Baum kept a 'Record of Failure' journal of all the rejection letters.

- Agatha Christie faced five years of rejection before her first book was published. Her book sales are now in excess of $2 billion. Only one author has outsold her – William Shakespeare.

You can't control what people think, so don't try to!

> "I went for years not finishing anything. Because, of course, when you finish something, you can be judged."
>
> *Erica Jong*

Commitment / time

However you look at it, writing a good book takes time. It's not just a case of writing it either. There's planning and editing too. Then there's hours spent researching agents and submitting to them in the hope of a traditional publisher signing it up, or hours spent learning the ropes of independent publishing. Everyone has busy lives. It's so easy to say, 'I'm too busy today. I'll write something tomorrow'. Combined with all the other factors already mentioned, carving time out of the day to spend time working on something that you're:

a) not being paid to do

b) have no idea whether it's any good, and

c) have no idea whether anyone will want to buy it when it's finished

is difficult and requires top levels of motivation and dedication. Many of the tips in this book relate to helping with this particular villain.

"The two most powerful warriors

are patience and time."

Leo Tolstoy

Indecision

Working hand-in-hand with overthinking, indecision is a real party pooper who can make it so difficult to make a decision and go with it.

'Is there a market for this book? Will anyone read it?'

'Which of my ideas for a book is better? Which one should I go with?'

'What narrative viewpoint should I use?'

'Should I write in the present or past tense?'

'How should I start my story?'

'What should I call the main characters?'

'What should the title of the book be?'

The questions can go on and on. So many decisions need to be made in order to even start writing a book, never mind complete it, overwhelm can easily keep you in a hamster's wheel of indecision. My experience of this leads me to say, just get started. Decisions you make aren't set in stone and can always be changed later. You can't change anything though if nothing exists in the first place.

> "Either write something worth reading
>
> or do something worth writing."
>
> *Benjamin Franklin*

Now that you've met the baddies that get in the way, I'd like to offer some tips to help you overcome them, at the key points in the story writing process: planning, starting to write, keeping going and once you've finished, so they don't stop you from writing your book.

Being a children's author has changed my life. It has enabled me to:

- See my books on sale worldwide online.

- See my books in window displays of book shops.

- Connect with people who've loved my books and been inspired by them.

- Get to the top of the Amazon category rankings.

- Receive hundreds of positive reviews.

- Go part time at work due to my book income.

- Earn money from doing something I love.

- Speak to children in schools about the joy of

books, reading and writing.

- Be featured in national magazines.
- Win the Theo Paphitis Small Business Sunday competition for my work as an authorpreneur.
- Have a book I've written translated into another language through a foreign rights deal.
- Be in control – writing what I like, when I like, working with people I like.

If I can do it, you can too! I hope you find my tips useful so you can get a flying start with writing your story, but remember that's what they are – tips. They're things I've found useful for my own writing, but they are certainly not rules. There are no rules for writing. Everyone does it their own way, and it's up to you to find what works for you. So with that in mind, read, consider and try out anything that feels right.

Part 1:
Planning Your Story

Prepare for Flight

"The moment you doubt whether you can fly, you cease forever to be able to do it."

J. M. Barrie

Some authors do not plan: they're *pantsers*, flying by the seat of their pants. They have an idea for a story and just start writing it, letting it develop as they write and seeing where it goes. Those who like to have more of a roadmap before starting a story (like me) are *planners*, or *plotters*. You might know that you're one or the other, maybe you're a bit of both, or maybe you don't know yet.

I'd say that I'm 80% plotter and 20% pantser. Whenever I've tried to write something without a plan, the story has run into problems. Sometimes I've been able to save them (by devising a plan), and sometimes not. I don't like to plan in too much detail e.g., chapter plans, as I enjoy it when the characters come to life and the story flows naturally, rather than having a very rigid plan. But for that to happen, I have to know some key things about the characters and main events. This isn't a detailed 'how to write a story' book, but if you're interested in learning my planning process, I'll let you know how you can at the end of the book. For now, here's 33 tips about things you can do *before, during and after* you write your story to prevent you running into roadblocks or getting ahead of yourself. For more information about being a plotter or a pantser, try the book, 'Take Off Your Pants' by Libbie Hawker.

1) Read With Purpose

Read and analyse the type of book that is similar to what you want to write. Notice the features, the viewpoint, the structure. Read like a writer. Observe why a chapter engaged you and made you want to keep reading, or why it's not pulling you in and you're getting bored. What makes an effective ending? What keeps you thinking about some books long after you've read them?

You're not doing this to copy other author's ideas or their style, but it's time well spent to find out what attracts you to certain stories and turns you off others. You need to be original, but it helps to learn from others. You'll be reading your own story A LOT, as well as writing it, so it's preferable to write in a style that you connect with as a reader.

It's also a good idea to read within the genre you're planning to write in, e.g., children's mystery books, adventure, crime, ghost, animal, sport, sci-fi, fantasy etc as it will help you learn the conventions of that genre which will arm you with a better understanding of reader expectations. It also allows you to see what's already being done so that you can approach the 'recipe' of your genre with a few fresh ingredients. That way you can deliver something readers will recognise but also appreciate a slightly different taste. This is what I did with my pony books. I love reading pony books, but as a life-long rider and horse owner, I can find elements in some of them rather unrealistic, which makes me roll my eyes! When I wrote my pony books, I wanted to avoid any eye-rolling, '*really?*' moments and present the stories and characters in a way that my ideal readers would recognise, relate to, and connect with. In the reviews I've received, many readers have commented on their appreciation of the authenticity of the stories, so my reading research has paid off!

2) Go for Five Stars

Look at reviews of children's books that are similar to the one you're planning to write on Amazon / Goodreads. For the four and five-star reviews, note what people comment on and what they enjoy or appreciate. Is there a pattern i.e., do you see the same things being praised? If so, that gives you some clues about what to include in your story. Do the same with one and two-star reviews. What problems have people commented on, or what do they think is missing? Knowing this, especially if it's something that's frequently commented on, will help you avoid it as you plan (or adjust the plan) your story and will improve your chances of writing a story that will be successful when it's published.

3) Know Your Ideal Reader

Sometimes writers think it will make their book more successful if they write something that will appeal to everyone. While it's true that some books have mass-market appeal, it's best to start off with someone a bit more specific in mind, such as boys aged 5–7 with an interest in sharks or girls aged 8–12 who love fairytale re-tellings. Knowing your ideal reader will help you focus on writing a book that they'd enjoy. That way, when it's published it's much easier to market it and your early readers – who are likely your target readers – will love it. It's been written for them after all. They'll tell their friends and word will spread, extending your audience beyond the ideal readers. My ideal readers for my Amber's Pony Tales series are girls aged 8–12 who have their own pony and are members of the Pony Club. They're riders with an interest in competing who are also concerned with making friends and keeping up with them, since their riding friends are often also their rivals at competitions. I have lots of readers who fit this ultra-specific ideal, but also many who don't. Six-year-olds who've never ridden a pony love them, as well as 66-year-olds who enjoy them for the nostalgia of their own childhood with ponies. That's great and I'm aware of it, but every time I write a new Amber's Pony Tales book, I like to get into the mindset of my ideal reader. Those readers really appreciate the connection they can make with the characters and events and even recognise themselves and people they know in the stories. That's how they become super-fans.

The opposite mistake is to write something unique that's never been done before. This may sound like a good idea, but you risk appealing to no-one. Yes, publishers and readers enjoy stories with originality but take care to make sure you don't end up with a lone wolf. Potential publishers will ask you to tell them which books yours are comparable to so they know how to market it. Readers often find books in shops by browsing in the genre section they usually read, and online by checking out the 'you may also like' recommendations linked to books they've enjoyed. If your book doesn't compare to anything else, it makes it difficult to classify, difficult to connect to other titles, and therefore difficult for readers to find it.

When readers enjoy a book, they look for others like it. They want to repeat the enjoyable experience they've just had. With children's books, it's often the parents who are the book buyers and they want to find something they're confident their child will like. Something that's very different is a risk, especially for younger readers, as it can put them off reading. I've had parents contact me to thank me for turning their reluctant reader into an engaged reader. And what do they do when they've finished reading through my series? They tell all their friends about it, then look for similar books to move on to. Now that the child has developed a reading habit and increased their stamina and confidence, parents want to keep their child reading so they look for more of the same. This is why knowing your genre and understanding your ideal reader is vital if you want to publish and sell your book. Comparable authors will bring readers to you!

There is space for you to record your reading reflections in the *Flying Start Stories Workbook*.

4) Start with an Idea you Can't Wait to Write

Part of imposter syndrome comes from being a reader and an admirer of stories. When you read a story you love, that makes a real impact on you, you think, '*Wow. I could never write a story like that.*' No, you couldn't. No-one could, except that author. This is because authors are made-up of their own life experiences, values, opinions, culture etc. No-one can write your book except you, because it's so personal to you. Think about your life and those of people you know, think about stories you've read or watched – true or fictional – think about what you care about. Watch / read the news to see what's going on in the world and / or your local area. Bring yourself into your story. I write about my pets – they're the main characters in my stories

– because I care about them so much and know them well. I don't have to invent personality traits for them because they demonstrate their personalities every day. I combine this 'reality' with stories I've read in books or seen in the news to create my fiction. There's nothing wrong with turning reality into fiction.

- What are you passionate about?
- What are you interested in?
- What do you really care about?
- What themes interest you? (e.g., jealousy, bullying, friendship, revenge, gender etc).
- What message would you like to put across to your readers?

Starting from here can help you come up with a story you *want* to write, enjoy writing and feel proud of when it's complete. If you prefer to write about something that is outside your own experience, I recommend considerable research into the subject before writing to avoid getting caught out.

Use the workbook to experiment with ideas. Write anything down that comes to you. Sometimes individual ideas are too small to support a whole book, but they might be a dot in a bigger picture. This means they may not work on their own, but when connected to other, seemingly unrelated ideas, they suddenly start to form something that comes to life. No idea is ever too stupid to write down. Think of a story as a complete outfit. You need several elements to make a perfect outfit: the top, the jacket, trousers / skirt, shoes, jewellery etc so you need a wardrobe of potential ideas ready to match up with other items. Some of them will work well together, some won't. You need to have them there though, so you can try them on and see which ones fit together.

5) Get to Know Your Characters and the View

There are two ways for authors to come up with ideas for stories:

- Plot first – This means they come up with the

storyline idea first. They know what the story will be about and what events will take place. Then they have to think of the characters to put into that story.

- Character first – This means they invent the character(s) first. They know those characters well – their strengths and weaknesses. Then they think of some events that will challenge the character(s).

In my stories, I plan character first, because I'm writing about real animals that I know well. I take the reality of their personality and relationships with each other, and think of situations I can put them in. These need to be things that will help the reader to explore who they are, get them to care about them and be interested enough in them to want to find out what happens in the story.

My *Amber's Pony Tales* series feature the ponies I had during my childhood. They're about the adventures I had with the ponies while I was growing up, and the lessons I learned from them. In these books, the ponies are important characters, but the stories are told from the viewpoint of Amber, the girl.

In my *Daley's Dog Tales* series, my dogs are the main characters. There are human characters too, but in these books, the stories are from the viewpoint of the dogs. This is something an author has to choose when writing a story – whose viewpoint will it be from? It can be something to experiment with to see which one works best for the story.

The first step I take when planning a new story is to think about the personality of the main character. This is important as the way the character thinks, speaks and reacts to things needs to match their personality so you don't have them doing things that don't fit with who they are. Their thoughts, actions and words need to be consistent and well matched to their personality, so it's important to make sure you as the writer know them inside out. You need to know their positive and negative personality traits, their likes, dislikes, and fears.

Think about the character that you're going to write about

and plan their personality. Remember, no-one is ever all good or all bad. Try to think of positive and negative personality traits as it makes a more realistic, relatable character. If you struggle to think of adjectives to describe personality, try Googling 'personality traits list'. I use 'The Positive Trait Thesaurus' and 'The Negative Trait Thesaurus' by Angela Ackerman and Becca Puglisi to help me and I'd recommend them.

It can also be helpful to consider *why* a character has certain personality traits. It may be influenced by genes, past experiences, other people, relationships, society, culture, and their environment. Planning this will help you know and understand your characters so that as you're writing, you can weave in little clues to allow the reader to get to know them and build their own impression of them. Readers love piecing together little details but you need to know your character like they're a real person you've known for years to do this, so take some time before you start to write to create every detail about them. Getting to know them well before you write a word will make the writing process much easier and your book will be much better because of it too. It's a win-win situation.

Use the workbook to plan your main character.

6) Know the Small Details

When you're thinking about a story idea, it's common to focus on the characters and events, but don't forget the small details. Before you start writing, decide *when* it's happening. This can mean when in history – present day or in the past – but also, what season is it? *Where* is it? Is it somewhere you know well and can describe authentically or a made-up place? If so, you need to know it like it's a real place. What's the timescale of the story: two days, two weeks, two years…?

Knowing these things will help you get the details right in descriptions and avoid contradictions that will confuse the reader. Using a timeline along with a plot plan can help with this and will make it easier to keep track of *when* you are in your story as well as *where* when you start writing.

Notice seasons: when do things happen, times of light changes, etc.

Be a magpie: notice things that could make an effective description or be an idea for a story. Listen to and watch people carefully for patterns of speech, intonation, vocab choices, catchphrases, mannerisms and body language, take pictures of things that catch your eye that could be an effective description in your book. Ideas are everywhere if you keep your eyes and ears open.

7) Be Memorable

Children are impressionable and books make a big, and often lasting impression. If you want your book to be memorable, rather than instantly forgettable, think about the impact you want yours to make. However, it's important not to be didactic. The author should be invisible; not preaching to the reader. It's through the character's mistakes / actions / reactions and what they learn about themselves or the world that the reader engages with the story. If you can, think about what's at the heart, or core, of your story, *before* you plan the characters and events. Which books that you read as a child have stuck with you? What are the ingredients that make them memorable? One of the most memorable books from my childhood was *The Hundred and One Dalmatians* by Dodie Smith. At the heart of this story is family. The dogs' family is broken by Cruella de'Vil the puppy kidnapper, and the Dearly family of dogs and humans is broken when Pongo and Missis leave their home to go in search of their missing pups. The book has *brilliant* main characters, a *wonderful* cast of supporting characters, constant tension and a pace that keeps you turning the pages. It's a pretty dark book for children, because of the contrast of cute innocent puppies with Cruella the villain and her intentions for them, but it also has lighter moments and well-judged humour. I used to read this book over and over as a child; I loved it so much and found the triumph of the good characters over the baddies and the families being reunited in the end brilliantly satisfying. Themes in the book are greed, power, family, friendship, teamwork and kindness.

Many years later, my book *Petra and the Dogs in Danger* definitely has elements inspired by *The Hundred and One Dalmatians* and *Watership Down*, another of my favourites. One of the reviews of the book from a reader said, "My son is 9 yrs old – he has a lower reading age and other special needs. He is not an avid reader and struggles to finish a book, but he was completely absorbed into this book. It kept him engaged throughout and he especially enjoyed the use of cliff hangers and suspense throughout. He loved the way the story flowed effortlessly into the next chapter, and we can't wait to hear about more adventures about these lovely dogs. I felt this book also highlights the current crisis on dog thefts in a way that children can understand without being frightened. My son feels this book would be great for all animal &

adventure readers." This gives me the impression that this little boy will remember Petra and her story and may read it more than once. He's also likely to read the other books in the series and he could even tell his friends about it.

8) Use a Recognised Story Structure

As a creative person, I hate the idea of following a formula to write a story. However, readers have expectations of what a story should contain. If these things are missing, it can lead to dissatisfaction or downright annoyance. As an author, you have to show an awareness of how stories work.

When I used to write without a plan, my stories were hard to write and usually got stuck somewhere. Now I have a method I use for all my stories which means I can write faster, I don't get stuck, my stories have twists and turns that readers enjoy, and I enjoy writing them as I have a guide to help me get from start to finish in a way that keeps readers turning the pages.

At the very least, having a three-act story (beginning, middle and end), also known as the Hero's Journey, is the basis for most fiction, including movies. There's also the five-act structure. This isn't the place to go into detail about these, but for more information, I'd recommend the book 'Into the Woods' by John Yorke.

There are several different ways you can plan a story, and different methods, or a combination of them work for different people. The three-act structure is available in the workbook. If you're looking for more support with this, it's something I can help with in my Head Start Boost short writing course. More details are available at the end of the book, in the Author's Note section.

Part 2:
Starting Your Story
Stretch your Wings

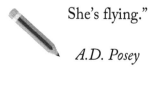

"Her words are her wings.

She's flying."

A.D. Posey

Formulating a plan to help you get to know your characters and plot can make getting started really exciting. You'll want to let the story that's brewing inside you get out onto the page.

But...I'll be honest with you. It can also be scary. Depending on the age you're writing for and the length of the story you're creating, the end can seem a long way off. It can be easy to dream about writing a book with the end in mind: seeing your published book, having it on sale, reading the reviews of happy readers...But before you can get to that point, there's all the work to do first. Thinking about the hours of unpaid work that goes into writing the first draft of a book, with no guarantee of success at the end can be overwhelming. There's also the pressure of writing an opening that will hook readers and keep them reading. With short attention spans and a world full of distractions, how on earth do you get their interest? It's no wonder that 97% of people who start writing a book, don't finish it.

You won't be one of them.

It's all do-able. I understand how it feels. I've been there. We're in this together and I'm here to help you. Here are my tips to help you face the dreaded blank page and get your first words on paper.

> "The secret to getting ahead is getting started. The secret to getting started is breaking your complex overwhelming tasks into small manageable tasks and then starting on the first one."
>
> *Mark Twain.*

9) Start as Far into the Story as You Can

If you've planned your story and have an idea of the narrative, decide where the best point is for the reader to enter the story so that you capture their interest. There are many ways you can begin a story, such as:

- Dialogue: begin with a character speaking to give an impression of who they are and what's going on. Let the reader work it out, based on what's being and said and how it's being said.

- Description: begin by placing the reader in time and place. Show them where the story is taking place, or show them the main character to create a strong first impression.

- Action: begin in the middle of something happening, then flash back to show what led to this event.

There are many other ways to start, but what you need to avoid is having four or five chapters of introduction and build up before anything happens. Don't start by showing your character living an ordinary life for six weeks before something changes. Readers won't wait. They'll get bored and move on, so think of a *scene* from your narrative plan that will be an engaging opening. Maybe it will hint at what's going to happen, maybe it will introduce a character's vulnerability or flaws to allow readers to identify with them. Perhaps it will introduce a sense of peril. It's likely to set up the expectations for the rest of the story in terms of setting, characters, genre, and tone. To write an effective first chapter, it really helps if you understand your story as a whole and that goes back to the importance of planning!

10) Experiment

Don't put pressure on yourself to write the perfect story opening at your first attempt. It's something that can be edited or completely changed later. Try writing a couple of different opening pages (or more even). You can experiment with things like narrative viewpoint and tense as well as different scenes. Which one lights you up the most and makes you want to keep writing? That's often a good indicator of which one to go with. Also, get feedback from your intended age group if possible. Which one do they prefer and why? Obviously, opinions can be subjective, so it's important to find out reasons for preference as they may help you decide. It can also be helpful to ask them what they liked about each option, what they didn't like or what wasn't clear and how they think it could be improved to make it better.

If you do this, don't worry about wasting the one(s) you write that you don't decide to use as the opening, as very often, they can still be used in the story, but elsewhere. Never delete anything you discount as it's very likely there will be a place for it in the story somewhere, or you may even change your mind later and decide to reinstate it.

11) Avoid the Info Dump

My first chapter's first draft is often awful, as it contains too much telling. This is why it's important not to put too much pressure on yourself to write an awesome first chapter straight away. The first chapter is not the place for an 'information dump' which means throwing information at the reader about setting and backstory. This is boring and too much to remember. Readers like to work this sort of thing out for themselves by being given clues, or breadcrumbs, throughout the story that they can piece together and build their understanding. It makes them feel clever and involved in the story.

This, again, is helped, by having a plan before you start to write, not only of what's going to happen, but of other things, like character profiles that detail their background, life experiences, family situation, etc.

If you find there's too much 'telling' in your first chapter, don't worry about it. Be aware of it and keep writing. You'll find places where you can weave that detail in throughout the story, so that it can be removed from the opening. Think of it as a placeholder for yourself.

12) Don't Aim for Perfection

This sounds like a strange tip, but as I've already mentioned, stories go through several rounds of editing before publication and the first chapter often has the most editing done to it to ensure it a) has sufficient 'hookiness' to pull a reader in and keep them interested, and b) connects to the rest of the story. I like to get a first chapter that feels good to me and makes me want to keep writing, then I just keep going and write the rest. Analysing a first chapter before anything else is written is likely to shut down the creative process, plus it isn't a good use of time. The time for perfecting is at the end when everything is done, not at the beginning. If you feel you have to perfect every chapter as you write it, that's such a burden and joy-killer. It makes it very hard to keep going and get anything done.

Just aim to write. Take the pressure off yourself and you may actually find that you produce more and better quality writing than you expect as you allow your creativity to push through.

"Rule one: you have to write. If you don't write,

nothing will happen."

Neil Gaiman.

Part 3:
Keep Going

Time to Soar

> "If you never dream of flying, then you'll
> never wake up with wings."
>
> *Natalie Kendall*

As you aim to start the hardest part of your writing journey — getting that first draft written so the story exists — this is where many of the gremlins get in the way In my experience as an independent author, I've found there are 10 steps to writing a book and getting it ready for publication (independently): Here are the first two:

1) Deciding what to write about and planning the story.

2) Writing the first draft.

Most writers don't get past step 2. They give up or get stuck during the first draft because writing good stories is hard, and the first draft is the hardest. If it were easy, everyone would do it. This section will help you keep going.

"A word after a word after a word is power."

Margaret Atwood

"Writing a first draft is a race to the death between your stock of confidence in your story and the time it takes to get the words out of your head and onto the page."

Piers Torday

13) Let it Flow

My advice is to write freely without analysing or attempting to edit as you go. Just let the words and ideas flow, knowing and accepting that it isn't perfect yet. Allow yourself to write imperfectly, knowing that you can go back and work on improvements later.

Flow is important to get the story done to help you keep track of where and when you are so that you maintain cohesion and avoid contradictions. Stopping and starting means you are likely to lose sight of the story's development and structure and so giving yourself permission to write without editing actually makes it easier to edit later.

Editing as you go can be a pointless task. As well as being demoralizing by making you lose confidence (because you see all the problems with your writing) it can also be a waste of time before the story is finished. You need to see what you've got at the end and understand what the strengths and weaknesses are before you try to go about fixing anything. It's better for you as a writer and better for the story not to edit as you go.

Imagination and creativity come from a different part of the brain to analysis and trying to do both at the same time is like attempting to drive a car with the handbrake on. It's a smoother drive if you just put your foot down and get on with it. Keep an eye on your destination, of course by consulting your map (story plan) as you go, but try to avoid parking until you get to the end!

14) Use a Writing Diary / Journal

As mentioned earlier, it can be difficult to keep track of where you are in the story. Even if you're attempting to write with flow, and don't keep breaking off to analyse your writing and try to improve it along the way, it can still be difficult for many to find regular and consistent blocks of time for writing, with no distractions. Life can get in the way! Having to take a break from writing for more than a couple of days, for whatever reason, can make it hard to get back into it. You'll have lost your flow and will have to re-read what you've written to remember where you are. By the time you've done this, the time you had available for writing is gone, and if you don't have any more time very soon, you'll be faced with the same problem next time. This is a common reason for stories being abandoned.

What I've found helps with this, as I try to fit writing around lots of other commitments, is to keep some sort of record. So, each time I write a chapter, I compose a summary of what happened in that chapter. I also record the *when* so I know whether two consecutive chapters are taking place on the same day, or if it's the next day or a week later, etc. That way, if I ever get interrupted from writing regularly, for whatever reason, I can glance at my summaries to get back into the story, without having to read the entire story again.

Even without long interruptions, I still find this a useful task to help me see how the story is developing and whether chapters are fitting together well. Also, if I've given a clue about something that needs to be explained later on, I can highlight it to remind myself of where it was placed in the story and what it was. It's just a little hack and though it takes a few minutes, I also find it useful for recapping what I've written, which helps me decide where to start the next chapter. You can find an example of this in the Flying Start Stories Workbook.

15) Make it a Habit

The best way to get into that state of flow with writing and blast through the first draft is to make writing a habit. There are often objections to this where people think they can't possibly make it a habit as they're so busy, they absolutely have no time to fit writing in regularly, let alone daily.

A word of warning: people who make that excuse are the ones who often don't finish their story. I've heard a great quote; I don't know who said it, but it says, "The difference between those who write great books and those who don't, is that the ones who do, didn't give up." Or something like that. Everyone is busy with their lives, and some more so than others, it's true. But when we look at the time we spend daily scrolling on social media, or watching YouTube or TV, or online shopping, or general browsing, it adds up. Often, we do these things because they're easy to do. We might be tired, and they require little effort, or it's a form of procrastination to put off what we 'should' be doing. Writing can be hard and requires mental preparation before it and full focus during it. The thought of the effort it is going to take makes it easy to put off and replace with some of our easier habits.

The definition of a habit is a regular tendency, practice or manner of behaviour which has become nearly or completely involuntary.

For a comprehensive look at the psychology of habits, how they form, how to break bad ones and how to use good ones to our advantage, I fully recommend the book *Atomic Habits* by James Clear. In summary, though, the behaviours that become habits are the enjoyable ones…the ones that are satisfying or that are immediately rewarded in some way e.g., they make us feel happier, more relaxed, better about ourselves.

You can develop a habit of writing by shifting your focus away from the difficult elements of it to the positive ones. Often when you sit and get started, you'll find the words tumbling out of you faster than you can write / type them.

Getting any writing done will make you feel successful, even if just in a small way. It may be that you're pleased with what you've written and you like it, or you may just have a sense of satisfaction that you didn't put it off; you got something done. This can build a positive mindset towards writing and towards yourself. You're a do-er. You're making it happen, even if it's a little at a time. If you associate writing with feeling satisfied, feeling that you've achieved something, you're more likely to return to it.

Some people form habits by setting small goals, such as 'I'll write for at least ten minutes a day. If it goes well, I may write more, but if it's not, at least I will have done something,' or, "I'll write at least 100 words," with the same proviso as above. This can work. Others get into the habit by scheduling a time for it each day. For some, this means the same time every day, but not everyone can fix their writing time like this for several reasons. You may need to look at your diary and work out where in the week

/ day you can timetable it in. By writing it down and making an appointment to write, you're much more likely to show up. If you want to get strict with yourself, you could even fine yourself if you don't turn up! Most of the tips I'm giving you are more *carrot* as you're doing this because you want to. It should be fun, enjoyable and give you pleasure, but it can be hard and if you give yourself the excuse of not writing because you're too busy / not in the mood etc, you'll never get it done. You know yourself and what motivates you. The *carrot* approach is my preferred method, but if you know that won't be enough for you, then adding some *stick* might just give you that added boot up the bum you need to get on with it!

I've now gone part time at work (I'm an English teacher as well as a writer), but I wrote my first four books while working full time. I also have three horses and two dogs to look after. My life is busy and finding time to write has been a struggle with a lot of late nights. I have to admit that the lockdown in 2020 helped as it gave me the opportunity to really get into an established writing routine. When I went back to work, I didn't have as much time for writing, but as I'd established the habit, it had become something I was used to doing every day, so I continued to write every day, as often as possible.

Being a teacher means work doesn't stay at work. There's always planning and marking that gets brought home, so it's difficult to separate my two jobs. To help me get organised, I use a planner where I block my time, so I know when I'm writing. At busy times, for example, when there's exam marking to do with a tight deadline, I'm not able to write as I don't have time and I wouldn't be able to concentrate on it knowing there are exams waiting for me. It's not always possible to write *every* day, but by looking for time, I make sure I do it as often as possible. It's not a case of finding *gaps* where you can fit it in, though. Unless you have lots of free time, you need to make the time. This means looking at your daily timetable and seeing what can be moved or removed to make space for writing.

Getting into the habit of writing can involve a bit of sacrifice and a lot of organisation. I do struggle with organisation, but without it, life just becomes too chaotic, and it's easy to slip back into making those excuses to give yourself permission to try again tomorrow. I am pretty motivated, but I have to be strict with myself to maintain the self-discipline needed to be a productive writer. As an indie author, I have no agent or publisher breathing down my neck and no deadlines to meet. Working without this sort of pressure really suits me as I'm a bit of a stress head about that kind of thing, but at the same time, that lack of pressure doesn't incentivise you to get on with it!

The best thing about being a writer is the flexibility. You can write when it works best for you. The trick is to not let flexible mean *occasional*, or *sporadic*. It's a bit of a juxtaposition to be flexible while also developing a habit to where it becomes something you do daily, but it can be done.

16) Reward Yourself

We prioritise immediate rewards over delayed rewards. A writer's ultimate reward is definitely delayed. We all dream of seeing our book in print, selling thousands of copies, receiving wonderful reviews from readers, and possibly getting a foreign rights or a TV deal, but these are all well in the future and are not guaranteed. They are certainly huge incentives, but unless we're highly self-motivated and disciplined, it can be hard to put in the work required for little or no immediate reward.

Writing a book can take months or even years of unpaid work with no guarantee of publication, success or earnings in the future. This is another huge reason for all those unfinished manuscripts out there. It's much easier to make writing a habit if we associate it with reward. Some of that reward can come in the feelings of accomplishment, as mentioned above, but we may need more than those intrinsic, personal rewards to really push on, especially when we're feeling tired, uninspired or under confident.

What can you use as extrinsic rewards for yourself? How can you pay yourself for your effort? Rewards help habits to stick.

Maybe for half an hour's writing, you can watch an hour-long episode of a programme you want to see. Perhaps for finishing a chapter, you get a soak in the bath with a nice drink of something! When you finish the entire book you can binge watch a series you've been saving up as a final reward. Choose whatever it is for you that you'll look forward to. For me, it's often free time outside. I'll complete my self-allocated task and then I know I'm done for the day, if I choose. I can do more if I'm in a good flow, but I know that once I've achieved my minimum, I can go and walk the dogs or go out for a ride on my horse. It's definitely a mistake to only write when you feel in the mood for it, or when you're feeling inspired, as writing is work and you don't always feel like it. If you want to get that book written, published and in readers' hands, you have to do the work even when you don't feel like it. Sometimes the words come easily, sometimes they don't. It's also worth noting that the ease with which the words flow doesn't necessarily correspond to your mood. You will find that sometimes you can be 'not in the mood' but when you make yourself do it, you write well. Equally, some days you may be up for it, but the words just won't come. It is easy to use the excuse of, "I'm not in the mood therefore I won't write well, so it's pointless doing it today," when actually, that isn't true. It is just another way to procrastinate.

Giving yourself rewards for your work can mean the difference between keeping going and giving up. You could even use a scale, such as:

- Bronze – if I write for ten minutes / 100 words, my reward will be X

- Silver – if I write for half an hour / 500 words, my reward will be Y

- Gold – if I write for an hour / 1000 words, my reward will be Z

You can adjust this according to whether you want it to be a daily, weekly or monthly target and how much of a challenge you want it to be. Apply the Goldilocks principle to your choices. If the reward is too generous for the level of work required, you'll make slower progress as there's little incentive to do more. If the reward is too difficult to reach, you'll give up. You need to get the work / reward balance just right . Try a few things out and see what works for you while accepting that some days will be more productive than others.

17) Make it Easy

Getting into a writing habit and rewarding yourself for getting words on paper are part of what keeps writers writing (or at least this writer!), but making things easier on yourself will help. How you can help yourself ignore those gremlins mentioned in the introduction:

- Overthinking / procrastinating.
- Perfectionism.

- Self-doubt / imposter syndrome.
- Commitment / time.
- Indecision.

Many of these have already been covered: write as quickly as you can, don't analyse or edit as you go, make writing a regular habit, and reward yourself for writing as this will help it become a habit that doesn't slip.

Other things you can do to make your writing life easier:

If you find yourself constantly distracted by your phone, put it in a drawer or turn it off during your writing time. Or if using a laptop or computer, just have your manuscript open and nothing else. Lots of open tabs will be distracting, even more so if notifications and emails keep popping up. Give yourself the best chance of concentrating on your words.

Have a variety of writing options available to help fit it around other things. For example, I have my manuscript on Word on my laptop (so I can work on it without opening the Internet and being distracted) but I also have it saved on Google Drive too. This means I can access it on my phone. If I ever find myself hit by inspiration when I'm away from my laptop, or I have some time to fill, such as in a waiting room, I can access my story via my phone to do a little bit. I've often opened my phone to write a sentence or two and ended up with a whole page! I think because the phone is often associated with relaxation and entertainment, it doesn't feel like 'work' to write on the phone like it does on the laptop. Maybe that's my weird psychology! If it's not possible to get on my phone or laptop to write, I handwrite into a notebook. Later on, I use the Otter app to transcribe what I've written and copy and paste it into the manuscript. It then needs checked for spelling and punctuation, but it's much quicker than having to type it all up, word for word. These little things mean I can get some writing done wherever I am and however I'm feeling. If I'm tired and not in the mood to sit at the table and type, I can lie on the sofa, or sit outside, and do a little (which often turns into more than I expected) using other methods. Find what works for you to take advantage of any opportunities for writing, no matter where you are or how long you have.

18) Get Over Yourself

I mean this with absolute love. Stop comparing yourself to other authors. Imposter syndrome is real and is one of the major obstacles that *all* writers face. There are so many brilliant authors out there to admire, and if you're a keen reader, you'll have author idols, I'm sure. Whether it's the success they've had, the unique and imaginative storylines they come up with, their writing style or the way they grip you and don't let you go until the last page that impresses you, and possibly intimidates you too, you're not alone in that feeling. All authors feel it, no matter what stage they're at in their career.

Imposter syndrome kept me from going after my dream of being an author until I was nearly 40! I'd always been in awe of authors and thought they were super clever, came from big cities and led exciting, action-packed lives.

I felt I was too ordinary and definitely not clever enough to be a writer. Who'd want to read books I'd written when there's all those other big-name authors out there, with movies made from their books? This links back to what I said earlier about having an ideal reader. My *ideal readers* want to read my books. They love my books! That's how I deal with the imposter syndrome gremlin when it gets out of its box. I *know* I'm not J. R. R. Tolkien or J.K. Rowling, but that's ok. Nobody else could write my books as they come from my experiences — my heart and soul. Other authors aren't competitors, even if they're in the same genre, as readers want to find as many authors as possible that they love. If you can think of authors as comrades rather than competitors, it really helps to avoid 'comparisonitis'. Just stay in your own lane, focus on your own writing, your ideal reader, and don't worry about what other writers are doing. Look to your idols for inspiration, learn from them, but don't try to copy them and don't put them on a pedestal. Yes, they're no doubt highly talented, but they will also be successful because they've worked hard at their craft, dedicated hours of writing time to develop their skills, and are further along than you are now. Remember, they started out with no publisher, no book and no readers too.

The final thing to say about this is on the topic of reading while you're writing something. In one way, I think that reading other author's books while you have a work-in-progress on the go is good for you as I'm convinced that being exposed to good quality writing is like eating good quality food. It nourishes your imagination and gets you in good shape for writing. You don't *copy,* but the influence is there, and reading can help to shape your own style. On the other hand, I've found that reading brilliant books can have the opposite effect. When I read a perfect, published book, and return to my first draft, the difference is so pronounced, I could cry. I could give up. It makes me feel absolutely useless. But then I give myself a talking to. The reason the book I've read is so much better than what I'm writing is because it's in its final, published form. It's been edited. It's probably had several rounds of editing and improvement, while mine is still messy, imperfect and hasn't grown up yet. It's like a teenage girl with spots, braces and frizzy hair (that was me) comparing herself to a Hollywood actress who's been styled, dressed and made-up by professionals, and wondering why she doesn't look like that.

So if you do that — read great books and weep over your efforts — STOP. Think of those published books as being camera ready. They're ready to be seen because they've been perfected as much as possible. It's the equivalent to being bathed, shaved, made-up, dressed up, jewellery on, hair done etc, compared to a first draft which hasn't even brushed its hair or cleaned its teeth yet. There's no comparison, so don't compare. One day your first draft will be polished to perfection too, but it's got to go through the ugly duckling phase before it gets there. Just push on and know that it's a stage ALL books go through, but it doesn't last forever.

19) Make Yourself Accountable

So often, when people find out I'm an author, they say things like, 'I've always wanted to write a book', 'I've started so many times', 'I've been writing this book off and on for X years.' Lots of people want to write a book, and many have tried, but given up. I totally get it. It is so hard to keep going, for several reasons:

- Writers are usually isolated. We sit alone, working on our words, in a quiet space with little input from others. We can get lonely and if it's not going well, there's no-one to share the struggle with.

- There are so many distractions and other things that keep us busy, as mentioned already.

- There's no external motivation — well there is, but it's a long way off, and we don't even know if our book will get published when it's finished. It would be much easier to keep pushing on to write a story if there was a book deal in place, with a deadline, contract and a hefty advance. It's unlikely that's the situation you're in, though.

- Nobody knows you're writing a book, except maybe the other people who live in your house with you.

So, my advice is to:

a) Tell people you're writing a book.

b) Get some company while you're doing it.

Be brave and put it out there. Tell your family, friends and work colleagues. By telling people about it, you'll give yourself *accountability*. People will ask you how you're getting on with your book and that provides motivation to keep working on it. When you can honestly say you're actively writing and making progress, people will look at you with admiration because they know how hard it is. You will like that look. It will make you feel good!

You could go even further and post weekly, fortnightly or

monthly word counts on social media to show people where you're up to. You won't want to show people that you've only written 100 words in a month, so it's another good way to keep you writing regularly.

Another brilliant reason to share your writing goals / achievements online is that you're effectively beginning the launch of your book. By letting people know about it, you're marketing it. As people become aware of it, they'll be intrigued. If you like, you can ask them questions about decisions you're making to get them involved with the process. I've even approached schools and invited teachers to get their classes involved in writing a story with me by giving feedback as I'm going along. Teachers have loved it as a literacy activity, children have felt important at being asked their opinions, and anyone who's had an idea or suggestion taken on board and put into the story nearly bursts with excitement! And of course, they ask when the book is coming out as they can't wait to get a copy. Knowing there are readers ready and waiting for your book is one of the most motivating factors I've discovered.

Finally, as part of making yourself accountable, try to find another writer or a writing group where you can talk about your ideas, share problems, ask for advice or suggestions. It's amazing how quickly you can go from being completely baffled about how to proceed with a story / story plan to being completely unstuck just by talking to someone else who understands stories and the process of writing them. Hearing someone else's suggestions and thoughts can unlock the door by either giving you an idea you hadn't thought of or leading you to come up with a new or different idea you hadn't previously considered. Also, by having a writing buddy or group you can talk to regularly, you know they'll be asking about progress and where you're up to, so there's built in accountability there too. It's win-win!

Part 4:
The Finishing Line
Stay Grounded

"A bird sitting in a tree is never afraid of the branch breaking, because her trust is not in the branch, but in her own wings."

Author unknown

When you get to this point, by whatever means you've employed to inspire, motivate and reward yourself, you've done what only 3% of aspiring writers manage to do – you've completed your first draft! You are now like the main character in your story: you'll have battled antagonists, been on a journey, probably experienced some plot twists and come out the other end a different person to the one who sat down to a blank page some time ago. You've been through your own character arc during the course of your story. You may feel elated and full of energy at what you've achieved, or you may be absolutely exhausted. Whichever it is, be proud of yourself. You've stuck with it and got it done and you should never undermine that achievement. However, a finished first draft is not a complete, ready-to-publish book.

This is when writers visualise their book in bookshop windows and the urge to get that book published is strong. You must resist the desire to send your book out to agents or publishing it independently the minute it's finished, though. It's not ready and you'll be wasting your time. Stay grounded as there are a few more steps to take that are hugely important to set your book up for success and make all your effort so far worth it. You might have finished the race to get the story written, but here are my final tips to get you on the podium.

The remaining eight elements of preparing your book for publication are:

- Writing the second draft / self-editing.
- Working with an editor on the first pass.
- Having beta readers read the manuscript and offer feedback.
- Making further edits based on feedback from ideal readers.

- Working with an editor on the second pass.

- Working with the illustrator (if having illustrations).

- Proof-reading once all final changes have been made.

- Formatting the book ready for publication.

20) Leave it Alone

What? After all that effort, leave it alone?! Yes. This tip I learned from reading Stephen King's fantastic book, *On Writing*, and I've heard lots of writers share the same advice. I suggest changing the font of the writing so it's not the same as what you've been using and looking at for the last however long, and then print it out. Staple it, hole punch and bind it or paperclip the pages together, then put it in a drawer for at least two weeks. Longer if you can. Go on holiday. Start writing something else or just take a break and binge watch a series you've been saving as a reward for finishing your story. Do whatever you need to do to forget about your story.

Doing this allows you to come back to your story with fresh eyes (that's why I suggest changing the font — so it looks different to what you were used to). Read the story as a *reader*. Try to forget they're your words and just read the story. You can look for typos and punctuation errors etc, but at this stage, mainly evaluate the way the plot and characters develop. Notice what you think works well, and what doesn't. Which sentences are clunky, which bits might confuse a reader, where is there too much telling and not enough description to allow readers to build their own pictures and impressions, where is the pace too slow? When I do this first read through, I return to my writing journal and turn it into an editing plan. I don't try to fix as I read as this will slow down my experience of taking in the whole story too much, so I just underline or circle vocabulary choices I'm not happy about, clunky sentences that need work, or repeated words I've used that are jarring.

I might also make small corrections to SPAG (spelling,

punctuation, and grammar) on the manuscript, but they aren't the focus at this stage. Bigger issues to do with character and plot get recorded in the edit plan, as these need more consideration in terms of fitting elements together and consistency across the story. You can get my edit plan in the *Flying Start Stories Workbook*.

21) Start at the Start with Editing

Once you have an edit plan, in theory you can edit the story in any order, but I find it most beneficial to go back to the start and work through chronologically to ensure consistency and seamless development. The opening three chapters are so important to hook readers (and agents if you're going to be seeking traditional publishing), so I recommend you start there. If you didn't experiment with different options for your first chapter earlier in the process, you could try this now. You have the whole story so you may feel that you want to start with a scene from later on in the book and then use the rest of the story to show how it came about. Or you might want to introduce characters quicker and give the reader a sense of who they are from what they're saying and how they're saying it. Here's some samples from one of my books to give you an example:

Chapter 1 – VERSION 1

Hollyhill Farm was an ordinary farm, just like many others. The farmhouse was in the middle of a jigsaw of fields with a small river bordering one side. Despite its name, the farm was not on a hill, though it did have a splendid view of a mountain range, so that might be where the 'hill' in the name came from. The 'holly' part was obvious as there was an ancient holly tree beside the farmhouse, as tall as the building. It wasn't shaped like a Christmas tree, but it bore bright red berries right through the winter, giving it a festive appearance.

There were barns and a milking parlour for the cows and some outbuildings for the sheep when they were lambing. There were stables too, but no ponies. The stables were full of old bikes, broken lawnmowers, almost empty tins of paint and other odds and ends that the farmer, Jim Burton, thought might come in handy one day.

It was a pretty farm; the house was painted white and at all times of the year, except deepest, darkest winter, it was decorated with bright flowers. They could be seen everywhere: in hanging baskets, old troughs, discarded boots and even unused milk urns. The farmer's wife, Heather, loved gardening and could turn just about any old unwanted item into a flower pot of some sort.

The yard was always swept until it was spotless, and apart from an assortment of cats and dogs who lay sprawled all over the place like dropped litter, there wasn't a thing out of place. Anyone and everyone who ever passed the farm commented on how lovely it was, what a wonderful place to live it must be, and weren't the animals who called this home so very lucky?

The cats and dogs, the hens, ducks and geese would have agreed with them as they were very happy with life at Hollyhill Farm. Sadly the same could not be said for the farm's herd of dairy cows or its flock of sheep. Both were so locked in jealousy and bitterness towards each other, they did not feel lucky at all.

Chapter 1 – VERSION 2

"Oh look, there they go," said Bramble, the head ewe, when Willow the collie appeared in the cows' field to round them up. "Getting taken inside for the evening to be pampered and cared for while we stay outside in the cold."

"That's right," said Bluebell.

"Totally unfair," agreed Bracken.

"They're the favourites. All this special treatment while we fend for ourselves," said Briar.

"Oh, not this again," said Maple, one of the cows who stood near the fence that divided the cows and sheep. "We don't get taken inside for pampering. We've told you before. We have to be milked since they take our calves away from us. At least you get to keep your lambs." Her tone invited no argument, but the sheep weren't to be outdone. "Rubbish," argued Bramble. "Your calves have nannies… baabysitters… a creche. You don't have to bother with them until they're older as the humans do all the work. Meanwhile, we often have twins, triplets even, and we have to look after them all by ourselves. Your lives are sooo much easier than ours."

"Hardly," said Mistletoe, the most senior cow in the herd, stepping over to join Maple. "You sheep need to stop complaining. You get lots of attention and help with your lambs, if needed. You get dipped and your fleeces sheared to keep you comfortable, and you're free all day long. You're just left to do what you like, whereas we have to be rounded up twice a day, every single day, to be milked. If the farmer has favourites, then yes, we're definitely more useful, but you ewes definitely have the better time."

"Oh yes, when it's raining and we're left out here while you're all cosy inside, we're having a fantastic time," grumbled Briar.

"Well…" started Mistletoe, but the argument was cut short by Willow, the sheep dog.

I sent these two openings off to be read by children in schools to see what they thought of the different styles. I was concerned that version 1 was too descriptive and that the conversation in version 2 may be more attention grabbing. However, all the feedback I received was that children preferred version 1 as they liked getting a picture of the farm and an idea of what the story was going to be about before anything happened. They found the conversation in version 2, with no lead up to it, confusing. So while a dialogue based opening might have intrigued older readers, for the age group this book is aimed at (6 – 9-year-olds), it didn't work.

It's completely up to you whether you wish to experiment, but whatever you do, don't delete any of your experiments. They will come in handy when you get to the feedback stage. I still used version 2 in the story, but it happens later in the story.

22) Keep the Overall Picture in Mind.

As you continue through the editing stage, do the big edits first, e.g., work on issues to do with structure, character and plot before you work on line edits. They are the final tidy up.

Once you've done your big edits and are happy that the story fits together, is well paced with a satisfying ending, you're ready for the final finishing touches. At this point, it's good to have another break from the manuscript if you can before you read it again. Now you're looking for the flaws at word and sentence level and for this second read, I recommend reading out loud as that's by far the best way to spot issues, as you will *hear* where the problems are.

23) Strip it Back

Writers often worry about word count. *Is it long enough? How long should it be?* We sometimes feel that longer is better, and often try to pad a story out, thinking this is what a reader wants. Readers don't care about word counts. Yes, for children's books, there is guidance on the number of words expected for different age groups, but it's not a hard and fast rule, and not something to get hung up about. It's more important that the story is told effectively, and this often means stripping things out in the edit, rather than adding things in.

In his book, *On Writing: A Memoir of the Craft* Stephen King introduces an editing strategy he calls "the 10% rule." After leaving the completed manuscript alone for a while to get some distance from it, he advises you to return to it and delete 10% per cent of it. But delete cleverly. Take out the unnecessary parts of your writing like needless adverbs, fillers, and excessive details. You can check out King's book (it's brilliant) and there's also an article online at https://writingcooperative.com/ from 17th July 2020 by Jude Hammal titled, *Use Stephen King's 10% Rule to Have a Sharply Edited Piece* that summarises his points on editing. He states that writing is about getting thoughts on paper. It can be a messy process, done in haste so as not to give words and ideas a chance to fly away from your mind. Editing is about sharpening your writing. It's slower and more analytical as it's about polishing and adjusting, so you're left with a clear, concise product. King says that writers should spend more time on editing than they do on writing.

This helped me enormously as I used to think editing was all about adding more to the story and fleshing it out. Sometimes it is — there can be elements of the story that my editor suggests going deeper into — but often it's about taking things out! It can be hard to accept when you see chunks of your story highlighted for removal (I had the first chapter of *The Second Best Pony* decimated by my editor – see below – which was a shock when I received it back and saw most of the first few pages crossed out!) but it's necessary to give the reader a smooth read where they can be fully invested and, at no time, are baffled or bored.

An example of the first edit of *The Second Best Pony*:

the new season to begin.

Amber had joined Blakefield Pony Club the previous year, but she'd had a disastrous time; being humiliated at her first rally; and getting eliminated from her debut round of show-jumping. And of course, there was the fun ride which had ended in disaster after a terrible accident. Amber reminisced, with the customary drop to her stomach, how her friend Joanne had nearly been killed after her pony, Flash, had bolted and tried to jump a barbed wire fence.

A sudden blast of chill April breeze sent an icy tingle down Amber's spine as she remembered that awful time, the fear that had almost paralysed her when she had discovered Flash lying tangled, cut and bleeding in the wire while Joanne lay trapped beneath him.

Thankfully, now eight months later, Joanne was nearly fully recovered and even had a new pony waiting for her when she was better. Amber missed her as she continued riding around on her own. The only other people she knew in the Pony Club were Matthew, Joanne's nine-year-old brother and Elisha Templeton whom Amber was distinctly unfond of. Elisha's family was wealthy - though her mother didn't work, and nobody seemed to know what her father did - and consequently she had the best of everything, including two top class competition ponies.

But that wasn't the problem. Amber had experienced feelings of jealousy last year, watching Elisha win every competition on her ponies, while she battled with

Amanda @ Let's Get Booked
Have not edited on this read through info dumping. It will be off putting to have not read the first book. I would shorten paragraph

Basically, anything that slows the pace of the book can be removed. Any 'info dumps' (seen above) can be cut by spreading the information out where necessary, and in brief, throughout the story to allow the reader to build their impressions of characters as they progress through the narrative. A good tip is to make sure you keep the original version of the manuscript, just in case you decide that something needs to be reinstated.

Remember, readers don't want fluff. It will bore them and

lose them. Every scene in your story should be either moving the plot on or developing a character. If it's not doing either of those things, it probably isn't needed.

24) Use a Professional Editor

After you've edited your story and got it into the best shape you can, I recommend working with a professional editor, even if you're going to query agents or traditional publishers. It can be tempting to miss this stage as editors are professionals and they obviously charge for their services, but to me, it's worth it. They are another pair of fresh eyes and can spot things you may have missed. They can also point out things that don't make sense to them or are confusing. They can spot holes or inconsistencies with the plot, and they notice things you won't have thought of. For example, I have a habit of slipping into the passive voice when I'm writing. Now, after ten books and having it pointed out by the editor frequently, I'm better at avoiding it, but to start with, I had no idea. When sentences were changed into active voice, it read so much better.

There are so many suggestions my editor has made about my stories, from the tense they're written in, to the actions of characters that have improved them. I feel that every penny of the investment was just that: an investment in my stories and my career as a writer. If your book is going out into the world with your name on it, you want it to be right, right?

If you're going to be querying agents, an edited submission is much more likely to get their attention (if the story is good, of course) and if you're looking to publish independently, you want your book to be indistinguishable from traditionally published books. There's a lot of competition out there so if you're looking for good reviews, or if you'd like to write more than one book, your readers will only come with you and read your other books if they trust you to give them a good reading experience. Readers won't forgive laziness, so that's why, especially at the beginning of your writing career, it's so beneficial to use an editor. I've learned a lot about writing from my editor and my writing has improved as a result. Now when I write, I can spot my own bad habits and things I know won't get past her, so they get taken out or changed straight away!

At first, I was nervous about working with an editor, as I felt I had to accept everything she suggested. This was because a) she's an experienced, professional editor and I was a beginner writer, b) seeing my manuscript at the start of an edit made me doubt my ability – it can be tough to see your work full of bits crossed out and comments about things to add in / take out / change – and c) I worried she'd be offended if I rejected anything she said. However, I've learned that working with an editor isn't about being told what to do, it's more of a conversation. I still have a mini confidence crisis every time I get my first edit back and see the work I still have to do, but it's also exciting to think 'here's my chance to make it even better.' I've trained myself to not react to comments as criticism or commands, but as suggestions. They are saying, 'what about this?' or 'might it be better if you did this?' or 'would meaning be clearer if you changed this?' etc. They're things for me to consider. I'm in control and I have a choice. Sometimes I immediately agree with a suggestion. Sometimes I need to think about it.   I may come to agree or I may have further questions to ask to help me decide. I may disagree. If I need to query anything or I disagree, I explain my thinking and we discuss it.

The editor is not there to be critical of you in a negative way. They are there to work with you and point things out they think will improve your book. Their career depends on the value they add as that's how they get referrals and repeat custom. They're your team and you can develop a very close relationship with them, especially if you work on several books with them. That's why it's important to find the right person to work with. I'm very lucky that my editor, Amanda, is an animal lover like me. She's a horse rider, owns her own horse, plus other pets, and worked as a veterinary nurse in a former life! As my books always feature animals, we're very much on the same page!

Ways you can find reputable editors:

- Reedsy – professional editors are listed here for you to browse and contact.

- Ask in Facebook groups for writers, such as the SPF Community group (self-published, hybrid and unpublished authors). Other authors will be keen to recommend editors they've enjoyed working with.

- The Alliance of Independent Authors (ALLi) have an Approved Services Partner Directory containing details of writing, editorial, design & formatting, production & distribution, marketing & promotion, courses and coaching and virtual assistant services for independent authors. See the guide here:

https://selfpublishingadvice.org/alli-self-publishing-services-directory/

- ALLi also have a Services Rating list where you can find a list of self-publishing services which are rated by Alli to help you identify the best and worst services for independent authors. Take a look at

https://selfpublishingadvice.org/best-self-publishing-services/

Most editors will do a free sample edit of a chapter or specified word count of your manuscript so you can get a feel for the way they work and the level of support you can expect. Editors will use this to get an idea of how much work your manuscript will require in terms of developmental editing (an in-depth edit of your entire manuscript) and copy editing (making sure a piece of writing is accurate, clear, correct and consistent). They will base their quote on this. If you query an editor and they don't offer you a free sample edit, ask them for one.

25) Use Beta Readers

In addition to getting an editor's eyes on your manuscript before you approach agents / publish independently, don't miss out on the opportunity to check the reaction of the ideal reader: the kids! It's all very well getting feedback from adults, but they aren't who the story is actually written for. Children will give their opinions with no holds barred, which gives you a good idea of how the story will be received. They'll let you know what they liked and what they didn't, which of course is useful, but one of the best things about getting kids to read your story is they're kids and you're not! They will let you know if any of your details don't reflect 21st century childhood accurately, or if your dialogue choices sound inauthentic.

Another benefit to using beta readers is that if / when your book comes out, you can thank them for their help and ask for a review.

It's important to think about what you want to know about your story. You can just ask people to read it and let you know what they thought of it, but then you risk getting vague and non-helpful comments like, 'it was really good,' or 'I liked it'. While this is nice, it doesn't do anything to help you see *what* was good about the book or where it could be improved. If you publish a mediocre book, you'll get middling to low ratings and reviews, which will mean your book will disappear when people are searching online. Online retailers push the books that sell well and have good reviews because they want to make money too. Don't waste the opportunity of finding out exactly what your book's strengths and weaknesses are.

I create a feedback form (I have it available in Word and on a Google Doc so readers can use whichever they're happiest with) which I give to my beta reader team, making it clear when the form needs to be returned. I usually give around three weeks to a month for this as the children who read for me generally need a parent to support with the feedback by talking to them about the story in relation to my questions and, often helping to record their answers in a way that makes sense. The parents are a brilliant part of the process, as they'll often give their thoughts on the story too, and even better, they'll let you know what their child's reaction to it was. When you get a feedback form returned that says something like, 'My child has loved it and wanted to keep reading every time we reached the end of a chapter. They've been telling all their friends about it at school, and we can't wait to read it again when it comes out,' it gives you great confidence for publishing the book.

I also get comments from parents about how it has raised their child's confidence with reading and general self-esteem as they've been made to feel important by the process. Their opinion matters. They love this. They also know they're going to be thanked in the acknowledgements and for a child, getting their name printed in a book is a big deal.

They're sworn to secrecy too. They can tell their friends that they're involved with me as a consultant and give them a brief idea of what the story is about, but they're not allowed to tell anyone what actually happens. They love this too! It gives them status and when they can show their friends the published book they helped with, which has their name in it to prove it, it's wonderful. I've had such lovely comments from the parents of my beta readers about what the experience has done for their child. It's a part of the process I really enjoy.

Here's an example of some of the questions I've used for readers:

1) Which version of Chapter 1 do you prefer? V1 or V2? Why?

2) How effective is this opening chapter in making you want to keep reading the story? What mark out of ten would you give?

3) What do you like about this chapter?

4) Is there anything you can think of that would make this chapter better?

5) After reading the first three chapters, what were

your first impressions of the story? How did you feel about reading on?

6) Is there anything that's unclear / doesn't make sense in the opening chapters?

7) Is there anything you can think of that would make these chapters better?

8) What mark out of ten would you give the final chapter? Is it a good end to the story? (A reason for the mark would be helpful too.)

9) After reading the full story, what elements of the story did you enjoy (and why)?

10) What was your favourite part of the story (and why)?

11) What did you think of MAIN CHARACTER'S NAME in the story? Did you like / dislike her? (please explain).

12) Who was your favourite character (or characters) in the story? Say why if you like!

13) Was there anything about the story that you did

not enjoy/understand/did not work/could be improved? Was there anything you felt was missing? (if so, what?).

14) The working title for this story is NAME OF BOOK. Having read the story, what is your opinion of this title? Do you have any alternative suggestions for a title for the story?

15) Overall, how much did you enjoy the full story? (A reason for your comment would be really helpful.)

16) How would you describe this book to someone who asked about it?

And finally, here's a real parent comment from one of my beta readers:

"Thank you so much for the opportunity to read your book. My son absolutely loved it – although he is 9, he has mild dyslexia and autism, so his reading age is a little lower than 9. He found the vocab manageable, and he didn't need as much help. He struggles with most school books to keep the momentum going to finish it, but he has not once lost this during his time reading your book."

26) Explore Publishing Options

You have a complete manuscript. It's been edited. It's been read by ideal readers. You might even have had a friend or relative (or professional) proofread it for you to check for any final errors that have been missed. Your story is ready to go out into the world – if that's what you want. Now you have to decide whether you want to go it alone and publish it independently or seek traditional publishing.

There are pros and cons to both, such as:

Traditional

PROS

- Prestige. It can be a huge confidence boost to get a publishing deal and your publisher / agent will help to get your book into bookshops, literary festivals etc.

- There will be no financial outlay required from you to get the book published.

- Traditionally published books are eligible for book awards.

- Traditional publishers will get your book into book stores, meaning you don't have to worry about distribution. Remember though, your book will only stay in book stores if it earns its place by selling well.

CONS

- It's very difficult to get an agent and therefore a publisher. You will get rejections and must be prepared for the patience, resilience and determination that are needed to keep querying.

- Your royalties will be less than you'd get if you publish independently and it's unlikely you'll be given an advance as a first-time author.

- The timeline for traditional publication is slow.

You may wait up to two years to see your book come out.

- You may not be consulted about the title, cover design, and illustrations for the book.

- Publishers generally do very little to market books. Marketing falls to the author, whichever route you take.

- You will only find out how your book is selling when you get paid your royalties every six months, so you won't be able to judge how effective your marketing efforts are in generating sales.

Independent

PROS

- You are in full control of every element of the book's content, design, publication date, and launch.

- You get more royalties.

- You can check your online sales daily to judge the

effectiveness of marketing activities.

- It's free to publish eBooks and paperbacks on Amazon and other online retailers.

- Printing is now available 'print on demand', meaning you don't need to order and store hundreds of your books. You can order as few or as many as you like if you intend to sell in person, or you can just let the online distributors take care of printing and shipping for you.

- It's the best route if you only have one or two books you want to write and publish on your own terms, just to get them out there.

- It can also be the best route if you intend to write several books as you keep all the rights. This then means you can sell translation rights, film rights etc, update covers whenever you choose, run giveaways to draw in new readers. You don't have to ask anyone's permission for anything you want to do.

CONS

- You will have to pay for editing (as mentioned), cover design and formatting unless you have the skills to do it yourself. It's vital your book looks exactly like traditional books, inside and out. It's definitely a false economy to 'make do'. If your book doesn't look professional, people won't buy it.

- If you intend to write more than one book and / or you want your book(s) to sell well and make money, you will need to become more than just a writer. Being an independent author effectively makes you an authorpreneur. There's a lot to learn about the business of books if you want to make it profitable.

Hybrid

Hybrid publishing is a third option. It's something of an *in-between* publishing model as it combines elements of traditional and independent publishing. Usually, a hybrid publisher functions like a traditional publisher, having their own teams of editors, designers and marketers. However, unlike a traditional publisher, hybrids require authors to pay for these services and are not given an advance on royalties.

PROS

- It's an option if you don't have time to pursue the traditional route or manage the independent route as you won't have to find your own freelance editor, designer, illustrator etc.

- It offers better royalties than traditional publishing. With a traditional publisher, authors get 8-10% for a paperback, and 25% for an ebook. Hybrid publishing can let the author take up to 50% in royalties.

- As you're not selling the book to a publisher, you keep the rights.

CONS

- It's expensive. This route is usually much more costly than using freelance services. You will have to take on a significant portion of the publishing bill, if not all of it, which is a financial risk. If things don't go to plan, you have very little recourse to recover your investment. Often, different packages are available but watch out for hidden costs such as buying your own ISBN.

- On top of having to pay out, you'll get less royalties than if you publish independently. Independent authors pay for their own services (and they don't have to scrimp to make it cheaper than the hybrid option), but they get to keep up to 70% of their royalties.

- A hybrid publisher has nothing to lose if your book doesn't sell as they're already being paid to publish it. A traditional publisher does not make back their investment unless the book sells. Some reputable hybrids will help to get your book into bookstores, but not all will. This is something you'd need to check.

It can seem exciting to be offered a publishing deal, even if you have to contribute partially or fully towards the costs. There are different models of hybrid contracts and it's very important to research prospective publishers carefully to ensure they are reputable. See Alli's Services Rating list, mentioned above, and the SoA's contract vetting service for members.

27) Join Author Groups

You don't have to wait until you've finished your book to do this. You may find it motivating to join an author group during the writing process. I've mentioned writing buddies / groups earlier on, but here, by 'author group', I mean an official organisation such as The Alliance of Independent Authors (ALLi) or The Society of Authors (SoA).

ALLi have membership levels for authors at each stage of their publishing journey including associate membership for those preparing to self-publish, and author membership for those who have published a book. They have a range of publications to answer your questions about publishing, and members also benefit from discounts on services, legal and business advice, rights licensing services, member forum, and their magazine. For more details, see their website:

https://www.allianceindependentauthors.org/

The Society of Authors is the UK trade union for all types of writers (traditionally published and self-published), illustrators and literary translators, at all stages of their careers. Members receive unlimited free advice on all aspects of the profession, including clause-by-clause contract vetting and a wide range of other offers.

I have found them to be very helpful and, as I do not have a literary agent, their assistance in vetting my contract with a publisher for the foreign rights to one of my books was invaluable. Through SoA, I am also a member of the SCBWI (The Society of Children's Book Writers & Illustrators) which is included as part of my subscription. This allows for connections with others in the children's book industry and attendance at events and conferences. For more details, see their website

https://societyofauthors.org/about-us

And that's the end of my words of wisdom. I hope you found them helpful. The writing experience is unique to everyone, and no two writers will have the same process, but these are my learnings since I began as a published author in 2019 and if anything in this book inspires you, motivates you or demystifies anything about how writers get from blank page to published book, then I'll be happy. Writing *Flying Start Stories* has certainly reminded me of a few things that have got pushed to the back of my mind, as there's definitely too much in there. I feel like a computer that's running out of memory and in need of an upgrade, so it's been useful to revisit some of the steps in preparation for my own future writing projects.

Go forth and write. Good luck and enjoy the process.

Helen

Hang on, I hear you say. The title of this book says there's 33 tips included, but I've only given you 27. Where are the rest?

BONUS:

EXTRA TIPS

FROM MY AUTHOR FRIENDS

Here's a little secret – once you are an author, you'll join an incredibly supportive community. Authors are not in competition with each other because readers don't read books by one writer only. Every single one of these authors has helped me in the past, whether it's by collaborating on promotions, giving advice or putting me in touch with people who can help me further. When I reached out to them to ask if they'd be interested in helping me again by providing a tip for my book, they were all happy to get involved. So, final tip (28) from me: don't be afraid of other authors! They're the ones who know what it's like and how hard it is. They're on the same page (ha ha!). Of course, there may be some you reach out to who don't respond, but don't let that put you off, as so many are willing to give advice and support to other authors.

Look for authors who write similar books to yours and read them. Get in touch and find your author friends! Just because you write alone doesn't mean you're on your own.

29) LYNN MANN

Lynn Mann is a British author from Shropshire, who, like me, has a long-standing involvement with horses. She was inspired to write her first book, The Horses Know, as a result of many years spent in the company of a very special blue-eyed, piebald mare. Her books combine the genres of equestrian, fantasy, dystopian and spiritual.

For more information about Lynn, her books and the horses who inspired them, please visit:

www.lynnmann.co.uk

I became an author because I learned so much from my horse, Pie, I couldn't contain it all. I tried writing a non-fiction account of our time together, but it didn't work – it felt very stilted and difficult – so I stopped writing. I then began writing a fictional story, a fantasy story with

Pie as the main character, and it just burst out of me and kept going almost by itself. It is with that experience in mind that I would advise any aspiring authors to write about what you love. I love reading books in the fantasy genre, and I love horses, Pie in particular. When I combined the two, I found myself not only enjoying my writing, but writing stories that other people wanted to read.

Once I had begun writing, I remembered a piece of advice I had read somewhere, telling writers to think about stories by their favourite authors, consider what it is exactly about the stories that they enjoy so much, and try to emulate those aspects when writing their own stories. My favourite authors are JK Rowling, because on almost every page there is a new detail, a new delight from her imagination, and epic fantasy author, Robin Hobb, who is a master at interweaving aspects of her stories into one another, and writing with such subtlety that I experience many "aha" moments when I figure out something to which she may have alluded some time before. I try to incorporate those aspects of their stories into my own writing, and it really helps me to enjoy the process!

I think the best tip I can give to anyone starting on their writing journey is to not judge your first draft. There is a saying that many authors, including me adhere to: "Don't get it right, get it written." In other words, whether you have plotted your story out beforehand, or whether you are a "pantser" (you write by the seat of your pants), give yourself a target word count to achieve in a set amount of time – I aim for 3,000 words in four hours but it can be anything, even a hundred words in an hour – and then just sit down and write without stopping to consider whether what you're writing is any good. Some of it won't be, but the chances are that much of it will be, or that there is at least something in what you have written that is exactly what is needed, and will spark more creativity within you.

I write all 90,000 odd words of a first draft before going back to do the first edit, and I usually have doubts as to whether it will be any good. Up until now at least, I've always been relieved to find that with tweaks here and there – some minor, some more substantial – the story works. This way of writing prevents many of the foes that plague writers (writer's block, procrastination, self-doubt, perfectionism and lack of time). Just get the story written and then go back and tweak it once you have all of it down – it will be better than you think.

Another tip for avoiding writer's block is to stop writing for the day while in the middle of a scene – it's a lot easier to pick the story back up the next day and run on with it. If by chance I have finished the previous day's work at the end of a scene, I'll go back and edit the punctuation of the last few paragraphs, a page even, and that eases me back into my writing mindset so I can carry on pushing ahead with the story.

Enjoy your writing journey. You never know what you'll discover about yourself in the process!

30) JEMMA HATT

Jemma Hatt is an award-winning children's author with readers around the world. Her books include 'The Adventurers Series'.

Growing up near Sevenoaks in South East England, Jemma developed a passion for reading and writing short stories, which ultimately led to a degree in English Literature from the University of Exeter. 'The Adventurers Series' was inspired by many family holidays to Devon and Cornwall as well as the mysteries of Ancient Egypt.

Find out more about Jemma and her books at

https://www.jemmahatt.com/

I feel very lucky to be doing this as a job and to create more stories. It's not something I will ever take for granted.

I've procrastinated at times. I started my first book quickly after I got the idea for it but had a break of about five years halfway through the first draft! I worried about *what if it wasn't good enough, what if people didn't like it?* But then I realised you just have to go with things. It doesn't matter if some people don't like it. That gave me the motivation to go back to my story and finish it.

Sometimes the thought of writing for hours on end is too much, so it's better to take it in chunks. When I had another day job, I drafted most of my third book in short chunks of time on the train. My tip is if you struggle to get motivated to write, set yourself a timer to write for twenty minutes. You'll be surprised at how much you can get done and will probably want to carry on!

31) NICOLA ROWLEY

Nicola J Rowley has worked in the media for 25+ years as a PR expert, journalist and author. Through her Communications Agency, NJRPR, she helps business owners and brands in the leisure and entertainment industries get seen through harnessing strategic storytelling. As an author,

Nicola's books include: The Power of PR (non-fiction), Mug the Wumph the Dancing Wizard, James and the Birthday Balloon and James and the Amazing Gift. Nicola lives in Surrey with her husband, son, and cockerpoo puppy called Rufus.

Find out more about Nicola at:

https://www.njrpr.com/

When it comes to writing a children's book, always make sure you have a PR and Marketing strategy in place so you know how you will reach those who will buy your book. You can write the most amazing story, but if no-one knows it exists, how will you make sales? Think about your ideal audience and readers and how you will reach them. This is just as important as writing your story. A great book without PR isn't going to be found and discovered in the same way.

32) MICHELLE HOLLAND

Michelle Holland is a qualified dog behaviourist and independent author of twelve books. She has a series of six books: The Adventures of Bella & Emily, which her own rescue pony, Chelsea, inspired her to write. Michelle's other series, 'Inside A Dog's Mind', are narrated by the dogs themselves.

'The Adventures of Bella & Emily' was a 2020 Equus Winnie Awards Winner in the Equine Young Adult Fiction category. You can receive chapters 1 & 2 of the book completely free. Visit:

https://pagimate.com/writers/michelle-holland-author

'Inside A Dog's Mind – Jacob's Journal' is also an award-winning book.

I would love to write full time, as I constantly have new stories going through my head, but owning my own cleaning company, helping rescue dogs in need, and having three of my own dogs and Chelsea the pony to look after, doesn't give me much time. Sometimes, I just jot a paragraph or two down and add to it as the ideas start to flow. Most evenings, I dream and tend to find a plot that I can add to my story, but need to remember to write it down before I forget! I love the initial part of creating a new book from a blank canvas. I would say the first chapter is always the hardest, but don't give up: write down what comes into your mind, let your words flow and you can worry about editing it later once you have more of the content. It's helpful to ask a friend to read through your draft; their feedback really helps, and their enthusiasm motivates you. Every single person can write a book, you just need to believe in yourself and go for it!

33) LEXI REES

Lexi was born in the Scottish Highlands but now lives 'down south' where she writes fun activity books and action-packed adventures for children, teaches creative writing, and runs a book club. She's passionate about developing a love of reading and writing in children and is honoured to be described by LoveReading4Kids as an "ambassador of children's literature." When she's not writing, she can usually be found outside, either horse riding, walking her dog or crafting.

Find out more about Lexi at https://lexirees.co.uk

I've been mulling over my tips since Helen asked me. When I do school visits, this question comes up in every assembly and my answers are easy – keep a notebook, try to write something every day, and edit edit edit (this is the point teachers like to hear most). But I wanted to go a little deeper with you guys and share some things I do which I find help me switch off my daily busy-ness so I can settle into a creative writing session.

The first thing is easy, I pour a cup of tea. What makes this unusual is I'm a coffee drinker, so for some reason I think the mug of tea tricks my brain into a reset! Second, I light a candle. This was a trick Derek Murphy suggested (if you haven't read his books on writing, I'd recommend them). Again, it's something I don't do often in my daily life. Derek also suggested wearing a "writer's hat". I haven't gone this far, but if I did, it would have to be Rincewind's hat, my favourite Terry Pratchett character. And as the final step, I put on a playlist. I know some people make a different playlist for every book, and I keep meaning to do that, but I just have the one. Hope that gives you some ideas. Please do send me pics of your writing hats!

"There comes a point in your life when you need to stop reading other people's books and write your own."

Albert Einstein

Recommended Reads

On Writing by Stephen King

Take off Your Pants by Libbie Hawker

The Anatomy of Story by John Truby

The Indie Author Mindset by Adam Croft

How to Self-Publish and Market a Children's Book
by Karen P Inglis

Writing Irresistible Kid Lit by Mary Kole

Into the Woods by John Truby

The Craft of Character by Mark Boutros

Save the Cat Writes a Novel by Jessica Brody

The Positive Trait Thesaurus by Angela Ackerman
& Becca Puglisi

The Negative Trait Thesaurus by Angela Ackerman
& Becca Puglisi

The Emotion Thesaurus by Angela
Ackerman & Becca Puglisi

About the Author

I'm a children's author, English teacher and former school librarian. My mission in life is to inspire young people to love reading and writing so that they have the literacy skills they need to access life's opportunities: being Lit Fit for Life! I love writing books for and *with* young people and introducing children to the book that turns them into a reader is one of the highlights of my job.

I run a Writers and Illustrators Club at my school, and I've led two groups to plan, write, edit and publish complete novels through a team-writing process. Current club members are working on a third book together, with members ranging in age from 11 to 18.

As a school librarian, I was involved with the Kids' Lit Quiz for many years. My team came third in the UK National Final in 2017 and won in 2019. They would have represented the UK in the 2020 World Final in New Zealand, had it not been cancelled because of Covid.

When I'm not reading, writing or teaching, I'll be busy at home in Cumbria looking after a variety of horses, dogs, ducks and geese! I'm a life-long animal lover and I often use my own pets as characters in my Amber's Pony Tales and Daley's Dog Tales books.

Find out more about me by visiting my website
www.helenharaldsen.co.uk

Author's Note

"At 30,000 feet up, the mind has plenty

of space to wander."

Eugene Redmond

A note about the title and cover of this book. Writers are often said to have their head in the clouds. This phrase has connotations of confusion, daydreaming, ignorance, being out of touch, or having unrealistic dreams. Writing involves daydreaming in the sense that writers need to think up and think about ideas for stories, and the process of getting ideas to connect and take shape as a full-length novel can be confusing. There can be a danger of getting stuck in those clouds, and I like the image of a bird cutting powerfully through the clouds and into the blue sky above them, where everything is clear. That's the image I had in my head when writing *Flying Start Stories* and it encapsulates the purpose of helping writers fly through the cloudy stages of indecision and confusion and into clear blue skies as quickly as possible.

For the sub-title, I worked with a blank space: ____ tips to help you plan... because I didn't know many there would end up being. I didn't want to set a number that would limit how many I'd include as I wanted to give as much advice as I could think of, but I did want it to be a number that ended in a 0 or a 5 as this seemed 'tidier' somehow than other numbers. So, when the final number ended up being 33, I was disappointed! I wondered if I could think of two more tips to take it up to 35, but when I read the manuscript, I really felt that the book was complete. It was going to have to stay at 33. That led me to research the number 33 and find out if there was anything significant about it. This is what I found:

33 is a master number and resonates with the energies of compassion, blessings, inspiration, honesty, discipline, and courage. 33 tells us that all things are possible and is

the number that symbolises guidance. It was fate! The book wanted to be 33 tips for a very good reason.

I really hope the guidance in this book is helpful to you and that you've finished reading it feeling inspired and motivated to start your book, or to return to one that's been abandoned. If so, a little review on Amazon would be very much appreciated.

I'd love to hear about your writing too, so if you'd like to get in touch with me, you could join my free 'Flying Start Stories' Facebook group. This is a group providing community, accountability support and advice for anyone who wants to write for children.

https://www.facebook.com/groups/flyingstartstories

You can also find me on Facebook and Instagram:

www.facebook.com/HaraldsenHelen and Instagram,
www.instagram.com/haraldsenhelen

If you'd like to have a go at using some of my tips, the *Flying Start Stories Workbook* is available to accompany this book, with space for you to start planning and writing your book. Get it in paperback from Amazon or as a free gift from me (as a downloadable PDF) by signing up to my mailing list at www.helenharaldsen.co.uk You'll receive the workbook plus regular newsletters where I'll share what I'm up to, my new book releases and details about writing challenges I run.

If you're looking for more support with writing your children's book, I'm here for you. I offer mentoring, Q & A calls and a short course, Head Start Boost, to help you come up with an idea, grow it, plan your narrative and start writing. This is a self-study package, perfect for those who want to get access to all the lessons straight away. You can work at your own pace and fit it around your other commitments. As well as the full course content of six pre-recorded videos, you also get a digital workbook to accompany each lesson and the exclusive Head Start Boost Facebook group which is just for course members. You'll have support and community from others who are actively engaged in writing their story and regular access to me.

For more details on my writing support, head to

https://www.helenharaldsen.co.uk/learn-with-me.html

Editor's Note

Hello readers. My name is Amanda. I run an author services website called Let's Get Booked and I've been Helen's editor from day one.

I can confirm that Helen was once like you. She was unsure and lacked confidence in herself and her ability as an author. It's normal to feel that way when you're starting your journey.

It's been an incredible experience watching her go from strength to strength as an author.

My mission is to help as many authors as possible to achieve their dreams. I want to help you on your journey by offering a special discount to Helen's readers.

I offer:

- Developmental and copy editing
- Book cover design
- Book formatting
- Book marketing design

You will get 10% off any of my services by quoting **HH Books** when you contact me.

Get in touch and let's begin your journey together!

www.letsgetbooked.com

Acknowledgements

I'd like to thank the authors who generously contributed their tips to this book: Lynn Mann, Jemma Hatt, Nicola Rowley, Michelle Holland and Lexi Rees. Being an author is a continuous learning process, and I've learned things about writing and the business of writing from all of these wonderful ladies.

Thank you to those who read the pre-publication manuscript of this book and provided excellent feedback to add the finishing touches: Kim Barton, Amanda Marshall, Denise Clarke, Karen Birchall, Iwona Vedral, Maria Langella Sorgie and Claire Tharby-Brown. Their contributions and suggestions were positive, supportive, and thoughtful; several of them have made it into the book.

Next, gratitude to the proofreaders who did the final checks for any sly little typos that may have slipped through the net! The fresh eyes of Martyn Robinson, Tina Redmayne and Dee Sturdy spotted a few sneaky errors trying hard to avoid detection!

And of course, my editor, Amanda Horan, who helped me shape this book, as always, through her thoughtful guidance. She is also responsible for the book's stunning cover, which I absolutely love.

Ingram Content Group UK Ltd.
Milton Keynes UK
UKHW020011150323
418546UK00013B/273